INCREASE YOUR WORD POWER

1

Woxbrandt / Kunze

BEAVER BOOKS

© **Beaver Books**   Dr. C. Kunze / B. Woxbrandt

Alle Rechte vorbehalten

All rights reserved. No part of this publication may be reproduced or utilized, in any forms or by any means, without the prior permission of the copyright holders and publishers.

Die Deutsche Bibliothek - CIP-Einheitsaufnahme

Woxbrandt, Barbro:
Increase your wordpower. - Frankfurt am Main : Beaver Books
NE: Kunze, Claus:

1. Intermediate. – 1996

ISBN 3 - 926686 - 23 - 5

BEAVER BOOKS, Marburger Str. 15, 60487 Frankfurt/Main
Tel. 069/774047 • Fax 069/704635

INCREASE YOUR WORDPOWER • 1

Animal Kingdom	**Semantic Field**	5
Born to be Wild		6
Back on the Farm		7
Cluster Club	**Word Game**	8
Wordpower Rockets		9
Over the Moon	**General Idioms**	10
Cool Collocations	**Lexical Structure: Collocation**	12
Euro Quiz	**Semantic Field**	14
Countries and Nationalities		15
Time for a Rhyme	**Pronunciation**	16
Rhyme Groups		17
Too many Cooks spoil the Broth!	**Proverbs**	18
Part & Parcel	**'A finger is part of a hand'**	20
The Art of Being Polite	**English in Everyday Situations**	22
How British are you?		23
Compose a Compound	**Word-formation: Compounds**	24
Synonyms	**Synonyms**	26
Mixed Bag Quiz	**General Vocabulary Test**	28
Link and Learn	**Word Game**	29
What's your Sport?	**Semantic Field**	30
Life is full of Ups and Downs	**Phrasal Verbs**	32
Homophones	**Pronunciation**	34
Find the Odd One Out!		35
Super Similes	**Idioms of Comparison**	36
Antonyms	**Antonyms**	38
What's Up?	**Phrasal Verbs**	40
In a Class of its Own	**Classification (Hypernyms)**	41
Shared Beginnings	**Word-formation: Compounds**	42
Famous Landmarks	**Semantic Field**	44
Straight from the Horse's Mouth	**Idioms involving Animals**	46
Look in the right Place	**Semantic Field**	48
Don't count your Chickens . . .	**Proverbs**	50
Look for Links	**'Day is to sun as night is to moon'**	52
Fill that Gap	**Word Game**	53
Sounds Interesting	**Pronunciation**	54
Vexing Vowels		55
It's how you say it	**English in Everyday Situations**	56
Scrabble	**Word Game**	58
Be as Good as your Word	**General Vocabulary Test**	60
Famous Last Words	**Word Games**	62

 NIMAL KINGDOM

Write down the names of these animals, then choose from the list below the names of their young; add your associations – the first thing that comes to your mind when you think of each animal. In some cases there are special words for the adult female and male animals, e.g. a female dog is a bitch.

Young: kitten • lamb • piglet • calf • duckling • foal • gosling • puppy • chicken
Female: cow • duck • mare • goose • sow • hen • ewe • cat • bitch
Male: gander • tom • boar • bull • drake • stallion • cock • ram

	ANIMAL	THEIR YOUNG	FEMALE	MALE	ASSOCIATION
1					
2					
3					
4					
5					
6					
7					
8					
9					

Born to be Wild

Match the animals on the left with the sounds on the right.
Each correct answer in this wild quiz scores 5 points.
Bonus points for acting out the sounds – 10 points per sound!

Lions	_____	chatter
Birds	_____	howl
Snakes	_____	trumpet
Elephants	_____	roar
Wolves	_____	hiss
Monkeys	_____	sing

Can you add any more wild animals to the list?

_____

_____

_____

_____

_____

Now match these groups of animals with the collective nouns on your right.

Many elephants	_____	make *a brood*
Many lions	_____	make *a swarm*
Many wolves	_____	make *a pride*
Many bees	_____	make *a flock*
Many sheep	_____	make *a pack*
Many hens	_____	make *a herd*

Back on the Farm

Match the animals on the left with the sounds on the right.

Sheep	_____	crow
Ducks	_____	hoot
Cows	_____	cackle
Pigs	_____	bleat
Horses	_____	hum
Cats	_____	moo
Dogs	_____	grunt
Cocks	_____	bark
Hens	_____	croak
Geese	_____	miaow
Owls	_____	quack
Bees	_____	honk
Frogs	_____	neigh

Which animals on this and the previous pages have

paws _____

fur _____

wings _____

tails _____

hooves _____

horns _____

beaks _____

CLUSTER CLUB

Divide into two teams. Group letters around the diphtongs to form words.
4 Letters = 2 Points; 5 = 3 Points; 6 = 4 Points; 7 = 5 Points; 8 = 6 Points; More = 10 Points

ea	ou	oa
ea	ou	oa
ea	ou	oa
ea	ou	oa
ea	ou	oa
ea	ou	oa
ea	ou	oa
ea	ou	oa
ea	ou	oa

Score: _____   **Score:** _____   **Score:** _____

★ Write sentences of your own involving at least ten of the words above.

Wordpower Rockets

Form words with the letters from the rocket. You can use each letter as many times as you wish.
3 Letters = 3 Points; 4 Letters = 4 Points; 5 Letters = 5 Points; 6 Letters = 6 Points; More = 10 Points; All: 20 Points

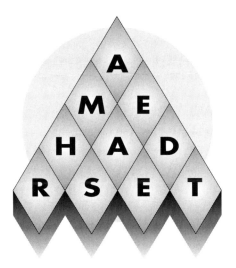

3 Letters

4 Letters

5 Letters

6 Letters

More

All Letters
D _ _ _ _ _ R

3 Letters

4 Letters

5 Letters

6 Letters

More

All Letters
_ _ T _ _ _ _ T

POINTS: **10** Take-off • **20** Try more boosters • **30** Gaining height • **40** In orbit • **50** Stratosphere • **60** Planet Genius!

OVER THE MOON

with English Idioms

'**To be over the moon**' is an **idiom** or **idiomatic expression:** an unusual combination of words, whose meaning you cannot understand from the individual words. The way in which idiomatic expressions are put together is often odd, illogical and sometimes even grammatically incorrect, but everybody understands them.

When you are *over the moon*, you

- have retired and don't have to work any more
- are very pleased or happy about something
- are over fifty
- have just reached a goal you never thought you'd reach

When you *beat about the bush*, you

- have been invited to a hunting game but don't know how to shoot so you stay in the bush
- talk about something in an indirect way without coming to the point
- wait for somebody to join you at the garden party

If you have to *pull your socks up*, you

- have to become more efficient
- have to wear socks
- have to dress more elegantly

If you *call it a day*, you

- think it has been a day to remember
- decide to bring something to an end or to stop
- decide to stop because it's getting dark outside and it's no longer daytime

Ray has *tied himself in knots*

- He's showing his flexibility
- He is confused, anxious and nervous
- He has worked too much
- Ray has a stomach ache

When you *jump a queue* you

- stand patiently in a line while waiting for something
- move nearer to the front of a queue so that you reach the front before it is your turn
- jump to a quick conclusion even though you don't know all the facts

If you get something *for a song*, you

- only get it if you sing a song
- get it cheaply
- you have to write and deliver a song to achieve something

The thief was caught *red-handed*

- He blushed when the police caught him in the act
- He was caught while committing the crime
- He wore red gloves when the police arrived

. . . .

If you *drop a brick*

- you say something tactless or inappropriate
- you have worked too hard at the building site
- you surprise somebody and cause embarrassment

. . . .

My wife has *green fingers*

- She is very good at investing dollars on the money market
- She is very good at gardening
- She is an excellent vegetarian cook

This man has been '*sent to Coventry*'

- He has started a new job
- People refuse to speak to him
- He is going to prison

TIME TO WRITE

Use the idioms you've just learnt to complete the sentences below.

1. I was _____ when I passed my driving test.

2. Don't _____, tell me what you really think.

3. If you are to keep your job you must really _____ _____ and work harder.

4. The burglar was _____ stealing paintings inside the millionaire's house.

5. I didn't realise his wife was so old, so I _____ _____ when I referred to her as his mother!

6. A year ago his beautiful garden was a field of weeds; Jim really has _____ .

7. Because we kept arguing my boyfriend and I decided to _____ and split up.

8. Do you mind if I _____ as my bus is due to arrive at any minute?

9. I bought the plate _____ as the shopkeeper didn't realise its value.

10. He was so nervous in the interview that he began to repeat answers and _____ .

11. When the boy behaved badly we decided to _____ _____ until he apologised.

Cool Collocations

| You can **have** | ○ influence | ✘ hunger | ○ patience | ○ a cold |

In English certain verbs are (almost) automatically associated with certain nouns: you can <u>have</u> influence or patience or a cold – but you cannot have hunger (you are hungry). These combinations are called collocations (from Latin: placing together) and are an important part of idiomatically correct English. The verb, of course, can have different meanings in various collocations.

Each of the following lines has three idiomatic collocations and one unacceptable combination. Mark (✘) the odd one out and explain the meaning of the correct collocations.

1. You can **ask**	○ a favour	○ an answer	○ the way	○ a question
2. You can **catch**	○ a bus	○ an idea	○ a cold	○ someone's eye
3. You can **collect**	○ information	○ stamps	○ friends	○ your thoughts
4. You can **wear**	○ a smile	○ a suit	○ a crown	○ an umbrella
5. You can **draw**	○ a conclusion	○ breath	○ an illusion	○ a picture
6. You can **lose**	○ a promise	○ your keys	○ patience	○ your way
7. You can **make**	○ plans	○ a promise	○ a journey	○ your homework
8. You can **pass**	○ the butter	○ a computer	○ a law	○ an examination
9. You can **pay**	○ a visit	○ attention	○ a bill	○ life
10. You can **play**	○ a party	○ cards	○ a game	○ the piano
11. You can **receive**	○ guests	○ an invitation	○ a letter	○ the measles
12. You can **see**	○ a doctor	○ the silence	○ the sights	○ a film
13. You can **take**	○ a walk	○ a photo	○ a haircut	○ control
14. You can **keep**	○ a question	○ a secret	○ your word	○ a promise
15. You can **hold**	○ an opinion	○ a promise	○ a meeting	○ your breath
16. You can **open**	○ a discussion	○ a shop	○ a door	○ a disappointment

EXERCISES

1. Choose ten collocations and write sentences to show that you have understood their meaning.

2. Because they share the same verb the acceptable combinations mostly also share a common central meaning; take some examples and define this core meaning.

3. Write down the <u>odd</u> nouns and combine them with verbs they are normally associated with.

1. _____   9. _____

2. _____   10. _____

3. _____   11. _____

4. _____   12. _____

5. _____   13. _____

6. _____   14. _____

7. _____   15. _____

8. _____   16. _____

EURO QUIZ

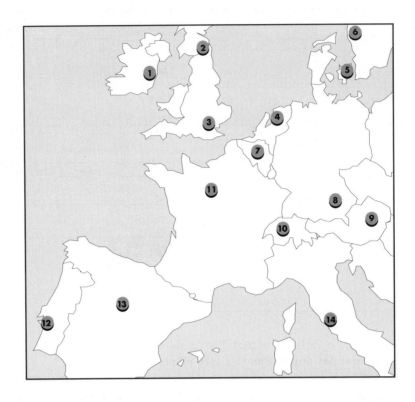

	CITY	COUNTRY	LANGUAGE	FIRST ASSOCIATION
1				
2				
3				
4				
5				
6				
7				
8				
9				
10				
11				
12				
13				
14				

1. _____ 2. _____ 3. _____

4. _____ 5. _____ 6. _____ 7. _____

1. **Which countries do these people come from?**

2. **Which countries are members of the European Union (there are 15 member states)?**

___

___

3. **Which of these countries have you been to or would you like to visit?**

___

___

___

___

4. **The cartoons above represent typical stereotypes of some countries: fixed images of how they are seen by others; write down stereotypes relating to European countries and nationalities. Are these stereotypes true / partly true / false? What stereotypes are there relating to your own country?**

___

___

___

___

___

___

TIME FOR A RHYME

Pair up the words that rhyme in each column!

1	post	_____	stain
2	break	_____	red
3	week	_____	choose
4	bread	_____	cost
5	heard	_____	won
6	rose	_____	hare
7	lose	_____	beer
8	cow	_____	hole
9	reign	_____	alive
10	flood	_____	lake
11	food	_____	chose
12	done	_____	speak
13	foul	_____	mud
14	lost	_____	plough
15	pear	_____	growl
16	hear	_____	word
17	five	_____	most
18	bowl	_____	mood

RHYME GROUPS

**All the words in the grey box rhyme with one of the words below.
Group the rhyming words together; then think of more rhyming words to fill the column**

ache	bird	blues	brake	brews	dear	deer	flair	flows	foal
gain	goal	goes	herd	lane	moose	pair	peer	pier	rein
role	shake	share	shoes	soul	stirred	take	toes	toll	train

BREAK	BOWL	HEARD	REIGN

PEAR	HEAR	ROSE	LOSE

Too Many Cooks...
...spoil the broth

Something went wrong with these proverbs. Pair them up correctly!

1. Like father _____ out of mind.
2. Love me _____ silence is golden.
3. Once bitten _____ ends well.
4. Strike _____ makes perfect.
5. A creaking door _____ keeps the doctor away.
6. Still waters _____ wait for no man.
7. Beauty _____ like son.
8. Out of sight _____ love my dog.
9. It takes all sorts _____ is better than none.
10. An apple a day _____ run deep.
11. Speech is silver _____ while the iron is hot.
12. Half a loaf _____ hangs longest.
13. All's well that _____ thicker than water.
14. Practice _____ is only skin deep.
15. Time and tide _____ to make a world.
16. Blood is _____ twice shy.

Can you guess what they mean? Give short explanations. Are there similar proverbs in your own language?

ROVERBS

It's never too late to mend
Don't put all your eggs in one basket
Absence makes the heart grow fonder
The proof of the pudding is in the eating
Don't cross a bridge until you come to it
Don't make a mountain out of a molehill
As you make your bed, so you must lie in it
Those who live in glass houses should not throw stones
The grass is always greener on the other side of the fence
It's too late to shut the stable door after the horse has bolted

Look at the proverbs which express in a few words a truth relating to everyday experience. Some proverbs are more easily understood than others. Can you relate the proverbs to the definitions below?

1. You can only prove something by putting it into action or use.

2. You must be held responsible for the consequences of your own actions however unpleasant they may be.

3. It is risky to concentrate all your hopes or money on one thing, for if this one thing is lost there will be nothing left.

4. Other people's lives or situations always seem better or more attractive than your own but may not really be so.

5. It's easy to say what should have been done to avoid failure after the failure has happened.

6. Don't worry about things until they happen.

7. It's never too late to improve or change your attitudes, behaviour or way of life.

8. If people are parted for a time they seem to appreciate each other more when they meet again.

9. You should not be too eager to criticize in others faults which you may have yourself.

10. Don't treat unimportant things as if they were important.

PART AND PARCEL

Pair up the words below with the ones in the grey box.

arm	book	flower	**hand**	ship
bed	church	foot	house	shirt
bird	computer	garden	leg	shoe
body	face	guitar	picture	tree

1. A thumb is part of _____**a hand**_____
2. A branch is part of _____
3. An arm is part of _____
4. An eye is part of _____
5. A wing is part of _____
6. An elbow is part of _____
7. An aisle is part of _____
8. A frame is part of _____
9. A toe is part of _____
10. A string is part of _____
11. A button is part of _____
12. A door is part of _____
13. A chip is part of _____
14. A mattress is part of _____
15. A flowerbed is part of _____
16. A page is part of _____
17. A sole is part of _____
18. A knee is part of _____
19. An anchor is part of _____
20. A petal is part of _____

TAKE PART IN THESE EXERCISES

Fill in the blanks using some of the words you have just paired up.

1. The front _____ of the _____ is made of solid oak and has an attractive old-fashioned brass knocker.

2. The rear _____ has a central _____ with shrubs and small trees. In the middle of the lawn there is an old apple _____ . In the autumn the _____ are full of fruit.

3. Your _____ is the part of your _____ which you use to hold things. It's at the end of your _____ and has four fingers and a _____ . The upper and lower halves of the arm are joined at the _____ .

4. There are five movable _____ at the end of your _____ . Your _____ , which you can bend, are halfway up your _____ , which can be used to stand on, to run, to walk etc.

5. James got down on his knees and proposed to Jenny. Unfortunately the _____ of his _____ showed big holes. Jenny, a neat and almost pedantic girl, also noticed there were several _____ missing from his _____ , so she declined his offer of marriage on the grounds of incompatibility.

Make a list of other objects, people and parts that belong to the words you have paired up.

_____

_____

_____

_____

_____

_____

_____

THE ART OF BEING POLITE

British people will forgive any number of grammatical mistakes but not the omission of the word 'please' or other polite idiomatic phrases. If you leave them out, you may sound impolite and rude even if you don't mean to be. Use the following words and phrases as often as possible!

MEETING SOMEONE	Good morning / Good afternoon / Good evening (polite, fairly formal expressions)	
	Hello (almost any time, less formal)	
	Hi (less formal than 'Hello', more common among young people)	
LEAVING	Goodbye (more formal)	
	Bye / Cheerio / See you (less formal)	
	Goodnight	
ASKING FOR HELP / INFORMATION	Excuse me, could you help me, please? I'm interested in . . .	
	Excuse me, do you know . . . / Excuse me, may I ask . . .?	
ASKING FAVOURS OR PERMISSION	Do you mind if . . .?	*No, not at all.*
	Excuse me, may I have some . . ., please?	*Certainly, here you are.*
	Could you pass . . ., please?	
	Would you mind if . . .?	*No, of course not.*
	Can / Could / May I have . . .please?	*Yes, of course.*
	Is it all right if . . .?	*No, I'm sorry . . .*
SAYING THANKS	Thanks / Thank you	*Not at all.*
	Thank you very much.	*That's quite all right.*
	Thank you, that's very kind of you.	*That's OK. Don't mention it.*
SAYING NO TACTFULLY	Thank you, but I'd rather . . .	
	Sorry, I'm not too keen on . . .	
APOLOGIZING	I'm afraid I have . . .	*That's (quite) all right.*
	I'm awfully sorry, but I seem to have . . .	*Oh, don't worry about that.*
	I do apologize / I'm ever so sorry.	*Oh, never mind about that.*
	Sorry / I'm sorry (bumping into someone)	*Sorry!*
	Remember: You can't use 'Excuse me' in the sense of 'I'm sorry'	
NOT HEARING WHAT SOMEONE SAID	I beg your pardon? / Sorry, but I missed that. / I'm afraid I didn't quite get that.	
	Remember: Don't use 'What?' or 'Please?' when you want somebody to repeat a sentence.	
OFFERING THINGS	Have a . . .	*Thanks / Thank you*
	Would you like . . . ?	*Thank you very much.*
	Can I help you?	*Thank you, that's very kind of you.*

HOW BRITISH ARE YOU?

Claudia is on a summer holiday language course in England and is staying with an English family. Can you help her in her conversation with her host mother by adding the correct replies to each sentence in the right-hand bottom column? Each correct reply gives 5 points. See score below.

1. Good morning, Claudia. Did you sleep well?	1. That's all right, but try to be punctual next time.
2. What would you like to drink?	2. Yes, here you are.
3. Could you pass the butter, please?	3. No, thank you. I'm fine.
4. Would you like some more toast?	4. I'm afraid I haven't. Sorry.
5. I'm afraid I have broken a cup. I'm sorry.	5. Yes, of course. Help yourself, there's plenty in the fridge.
6. May I have a front door key, please?	6. No, not at all, go ahead.
7. Is it all right if I come home a bit later tonight?	7. Tea, please.
8. May I borrow your dictionary?	8. Yes, thank you, very well.
9. Do you mind if I watch television?	9. Certainly, here you are.
10. May I have something to drink, please?	10. Oh, never mind about that, we'll replace it.
11. Have you got the time, please?	11. Yes, of course, but don't lose it!
12. I'm sorry I'm late.	12. Yes, all right, but be home by 10 o'clock.

1. Good morning, Claudia. Did you sleep well?   1. _____

2. What would you like to drink?   2. _____

3. Could you pass the butter, please?   3. _____

4. Would you like some more toast?   4. _____

5. I'm afraid I have broken a cup. I'm sorry.   5. _____

6. May I have a front door key, please?   6. _____

7. Is it all right if I come home a bit later tonight?   7. _____

8. May I borrow your dictionary?   8. _____

9. Do you mind if I watch television?   9. _____

10. May I have something to drink, please?   10. _____

11. Have you got the time, please?   11. _____

12. I'm sorry I'm late.   12. _____

SCORE:
- 60 - 55 You've made it. You're British!
- 50 - 40 Good effort. You're nearly there.
- 35 - 20 Read about good manners again.
- 15 - 00 You're definitely a foreigner!

COMPOSE A COMPOUND

Compounds are words that are made up of two words to express a new meaning: a blackboard, for example, is not just a black board (notice also the change in intonation), but is a new and independent word.
There are solid compounds, in which the formative words melt into one (blackboard, handbag) and open compounds (coffee cup, dining room), which may also be connected by a hyphen (self-service, free-range). Pair them up correctly.

SOLID COMPOUNDS ◆ OPEN COMPOUNDS

sky	paper	parking		office
black	point	car		call
house	shake	petrol		player
grand	way	pocket		park
race	copy	gold		flight
watch	horse	status		tennis
photo	dog	dance		money
motor	flake	ice		station
hand	quake	Prime		symbol
street	boat	tea		cube
news	lamp	junk		medal
school	scraper	CD		break
stand	stick	youth		floor
snow	cut	table		ticket
hair	bird	charter		food
lip	boy	registry		club
earth	father	phone		Minister

24

CHOOSE A COMPOUND

The text below contains compounds from the previous page. Fill in the missing parts of the compounds.

1. I woke on my house_____ to the sound of a _____bird singing.

2. The school_____ did not enjoy having a hair_____ .

3. The match ended with a _____shake and a gold _____ for the winner.

4. At the _____ club teenagers are able to play _____ tennis or have a disco on the dance _____ .

5. I need a _____copy of my birth certificate from the _____ office.

6. We left our car under a street_____ as the _____ park was full and sadly found a _____ ticket on our return.

7. I saved the _____ money my _____father gave me and eventually had enough to buy a C.D. _____ .

8. From my stand_____ our government should help the victims of the earth_____ immediately.

9. We stopped at a petrol _____ on the _____way.

10. Our _____dog barked when thieves tried to steal our valuable race_____ .

11. _____flakes began to settle on the runway and our charter _____ was delayed.

12. The _____ Minister received an important phone _____ in his office.

BEAUTIFUL FAIR PRETTY GOOD-LOOKING HANDSOME LOVELY

Synonyms

Synonyms are words which have the same meaning or nearly the same meaning.
For each word on the left there is a synonym in the right-hand column. Pair them up correctly.

brave	_____	cautious	1	disappear _____	respect
stubborn	_____	correct	2	loathe _____	respond
insane	_____	pertinent	3	alter _____	deceive
mean	_____	keen	4	boast _____	adore
giddy	_____	lucky	5	hide _____	observe
firm	_____	enormous	6	help _____	vanish
eager	_____	sacred	7	love _____	cease
strong	_____	mad	8	answer _____	change
fortunate	_____	obstinate	9	admire _____	strike
holy	_____	courageous	10	beat _____	construct
relevant	_____	dizzy	11	look _____	defeat
right	_____	powerful	12	hit _____	conceal
huge	_____	tidy	13	swindle _____	detest
neat	_____	stingy	14	build _____	brag
careful	_____	solid	15	finish _____	assist

SYNONYM QUARTETS

**Synonyms are words that mean the same or nearly the same as another.
Pair up the synonyms in the grey box with their partners below; explain what central meaning they share.**

| arrangement | arrogance | boundary | dislike | happiness | harmony | misfortune | outcome |
| pain | present | quarrel | risk | support | talk | **tenderness** | untruth |

1. love, affection, fondness ____**tenderness**____   9. chat, conversation, conference _____

2. peace, agreement, unity _____   10. contentment, bliss, pleasure _____

3. aid, help, protection _____   11. hatred, ill will, enmity _____

4. agreement, contract, deal _____   12. gift, grant, donation _____

5. danger, hazard, peril _____   13. fight, row, brawl _____

6. lie, falsehood, deception _____   14. bad luck, catastrophe, harm _____

7. consequence, effect, result _____   15. ache, distress, suffering _____

8. barrier, border, frontier _____   16. vanity, pride, conceit _____

Now choose one of the synonyms from each group and use it to make a sentence.

_____
_____
_____
_____
_____
_____
_____
_____

27

MIXED BAG QUIZ

Read the alternatives and when you think you know the corrrect answer, tick the appropriate box.

A large store is divided into . .
- ○ departments
- ○ divisions
- ○ units
- ○ compartments

An American calls it a bill; in Britain it is
- ○ a banknote
- ○ cash
- ○ a cheque
- ○ a coin

When two colours go with each other, they . .
- ○ suit
- ○ match
- ○ pass
- ○ fit

A person who is hopeful about the future is
- ○ a pessimist
- ○ a realist
- ○ a spendthrift
- ○ an optimist

The place where a river starts is its
- ○ estuary
- ○ source
- ○ beginning
- ○ origin

The water in your mouth is called
- ○ sweat
- ○ perspiration
- ○ mouthwash
- ○ saliva

Which word cannot describe someone who is old?
- ○ elderly
- ○ aged
- ○ senile
- ○ antique

Angry people sometimes _____ their teeth.
- ○ curl
- ○ clench
- ○ screw up
- ○ hack

When people meet again after a long time, it's
- ○ a reception
- ○ a recommendation
- ○ a reunion
- ○ a reconciliation

I hate doing my _____ - especially maths.
- ○ homework
- ○ housework
- ○ hometraining
- ○ home time

The two holes in the nose are called
- ○ ventilators
- ○ funnels
- ○ nostrils
- ○ shafts

If you hear of the late Mr May, you know he is
- ○ never punctual
- ○ sometimes late
- ○ dead
- ○ always late

The words depth, height and width all have something to do with
- ○ sports
- ○ measurement
- ○ shapes
- ○ lines

Tom drank too much last night. Now he has a
- ○ headlock
- ○ brainwave
- ○ brainstorm
- ○ hangover

The time between night and day is called
- ○ dawn
- ○ brightness
- ○ glow
- ○ lighting

Which word means well-known in a negative way?
- ○ famous
- ○ eminent
- ○ celebrated
- ○ notorious

How would you describe this facial expression?
- ○ a smile
- ○ a twinkle
- ○ a grin
- ○ a smirk

 Link and Learn

**Form words by linking the letters. You can use each letter as often as you wish.
Start anywhere; you can go in all directions: left, right, up, down or diagonally**

3 Letters = 1 Point; 4 Letters = 2 Points; 5 Letters = 4 Points; 6 Letters = 6 Points; More = 10 Points

H	E	Y	R	T
T	E	A	S	L
E	S	S	E	B
N	Y	R	I	K
O	M	G	C	S

B	I	R	A	T
L	O	T	H	N
A	N	R	D	E
D	T	Y	A	R
O	M	E	P	S

3 Letters _____

4 Letters _____

5 Letters _____

6 Letters _____

More _____

SCORE: _____

3 Letters _____

4 Letters _____

5 Letters _____

6 Letters _____

More _____

SCORE: _____

WHAT'S YOUR SPORT?

Sort Out the Sport!

Look at the illustrations. Then write down the name of the sport below. Some of the words in the next column may help you.

Relate the words in the box to the sports mentioned below. Write them down under the sport you normally associate them with. You can use some of the words more than once.

air tank	glove	pole	shin guard
ballboy	hat	racquet	ski
bar	helmet	reins	skiing goggles
bat	lane	ring	stirrup
boots	mask	saddle	track
flipper	net	serve	wet suit

1. _____
2. _____
3. _____
4. _____
5. _____
6. _____
7. _____
8. _____
9. _____
10. _____
11. _____
12. _____
13. _____
14. _____

Riding: _____

Athletics: _____

Tennis: _____

Skiing: _____

Scuba diving: _____

Baseball: _____

Divide the sports into

team games _____

water sports _____

aerial sports _____

winter sports _____

equestrian sports _____

athletics _____

combat sports _____

Life is full of
Ups and Downs

It is easy to understand 'up the stairs, up in the sky', but there are many phrasal verbs (verb + adverb or preposition) with UP with an idiomatic meaning all of their own as in They broke up (separated) or He turned up (came, appeared). Complete the sentences below with the verbs in the grey box.

| chop | cut | do | eat | give | hush | keep | let | sell | slow | talk | track |

1. The Mays are emigrating to Australia and are _____ up their shop.

2. You promised to come with me! You can't just _____ me down now.

3. _____ up your dinner first, then you'll get some ice cream.

4. You must _____ down on alcohol and fat, if you've got high blood pressure.

5. The police managed to _____ down the escaped prisoner in a small wood.

6. I'll be ready in a second. I just have to _____ up my shoe laces.

7. Don't _____ up. There is still hope that you get that job.

8. _____ down! You're driving much too fast.

9. They tried to _____ up the scandal, but of course it all came out in the end.

10. Don't _____ down to me as if I was a child.

11. If this rainy weather _____ up, we will get a very bad harvest.

12. It's a pity that they had to _____ down that lovely tree.

PAIR THEM UP AND WRITE THEM DOWN

Write down the phrasals with 'up' and 'down' next to their explanations below.

blow up • break down • dress up • get up • grow up • play down
settle down • slip up • turn down • wash up • wind down • write down

explode _____   describe as less important _____

wear smarter clothes than usual _____   put it into written form _____

get out of bed _____   relax _____

clean the dishes _____   stop functioning _____

become adult _____   refuse _____

make a mistake _____   make oneself comfortable _____

Choose from phrasals on these pages and write sentences to show that you've understood their meaning.

_____
_____
_____
_____
_____
_____
_____
_____
_____
_____
_____
_____

...Dear Diary, reigned all day yesterday, reigning again today

Homophones

A homophone (from Greek 'homo'=same and phoné=sound) is a word which sounds the same as another word, but is spelt differently and has a different meaning, the verbs 'to reign' and 'to rain' are homophones. Pair up the words in the grey box with the words below to make homophone pairs.

bare	blue	brake	by	eight	flour	hair	hear	heard	knot
mail	new	nose	plain	scene	son	two	weak	won	write

ate _____ flower _____ knows _____ right _____

bear _____ hare _____ male _____ seen _____

blew _____ herd _____ not _____ sun _____

break _____ here _____ one _____ too _____

buy _____ knew _____ plane _____ week _____

Fill in the blanks using the homophone pairs from above; you must use both words in each sentence

1. I can't _____ my husband walking in his _____ feet indoors.

2. Luckily the garage fixed the faulty _____ during my lunch _____ .

3. Everybody _____ that Jim has always got his _____ in a book.

4. He _____ that my dress was _____ but he didn't say anything.

5. Liverpool _____ the match by _____ to nil.

6. I kept telling my teenage _____ to stay out of the _____ but he wouldn't listen. _____ tomorrow morning he will have to _____ himself some nice, soothing lotion!

ODD ONE OUT!

Find the word that doesn't rhyme with the other three!

1	2	3	4
○ bow	○ bread	○ done	○ made
○ cow	○ shed	○ one	○ shade
○ sew	○ led	○ won	○ said
○ blow	○ greed	○ bone	○ maid
○ food	○ no	○ goes	○ load
○ hood	○ so	○ does	○ broad
○ sued	○ to	○ mows	○ mowed
○ rude	○ know	○ close	○ rode
○ coal	○ bird	○ bed	○ pair
○ foul	○ heard	○ bead	○ pear
○ soul	○ ford	○ dead	○ peer
○ roll	○ word	○ bread	○ dare
○ bake	○ crown	○ great	○ meat
○ brake	○ flown	○ late	○ heat
○ beak	○ noun	○ greet	○ threat
○ break	○ clown	○ grate	○ sweet
○ know	○ bun	○ tough	○ flower
○ now	○ son	○ though	○ flour
○ toe	○ gone	○ enough	○ power
○ low	○ done	○ rough	○ lower
○ heart	○ through	○ rose	○ foul
○ heard	○ cough	○ chose	○ bowl
○ hart	○ shoe	○ choose	○ owl
○ cart	○ flew	○ goes	○ growl

35

Super Similes

*E*nglish is rich in similes which make the conversation more lively and clear. Similes are expressions which describe a person or thing as being similar to someone or something else, e.g. *'He's as white as a sheet'*. Similes usually start with the word *'as'*.

1. _____
2. _____
3. _____
4. _____
5. _____
6. _____
7. _____
8. _____
9. _____
10. _____

Divide into two teams. Write down the names of the animals and objects in the box above. You get 5 points for each correct answer. Then pair them up with the following words to make similes like *'As wise as an owl'*. You get an additional 10 points for each correct answer.

clear • free • good • light • poor • pretty • quick • sober • strong • thin

1. As _____ as a _____
2. As _____ as a _____
3. As _____ as _____
4. As _____ as _____
5. As _____ as a _____
6. As _____ as a _____
7. As _____ as a _____
8. As _____ as a _____
9. As _____ as a _____
10. As _____ as a _____

Total score: _____

More Similes

Pair up the adjectives on the left-hand side with the nouns on the right to make some more similes.

Choose suitable phrases from above to completes the sentences below.

1. A nail punctured the tyre of my bicycle. Now my tyre is as _____ .

2. If you want to speak to my mother you'll have to shout! She's as _____ .

3. You wouldn't believe that Ann and Diann are sisters, would you? They're as _____

   _____ . Their brothers, Ian and John, however,

   are as _____ .

4. I've heard that joke a hundred times at least. It's as _____ .

5. Where have they all gone? It's as _____ in here.

6. Why don't you cheer up? You've been as _____ for the past two days!

7. He was very nervous when signing the document, but his hand was as _____ .

8. The morning after the party we were all exhausted except Diann, who was as _____

   _____ .

9. Don't expect any sympathy from my father – he's as _____ .

10. He'll live for many years to come. He's as _____ .

11. I'm not worried about the weather. My new coat keeps me as _____ .

ANTONYMS

An antonym is a word which means the opposite, or nearly the opposite, of another word.
Complete the wheels below by adding the correct antonyms at the opposite ends of the arrows;
then use the antonym pairs to complete the sentences below.

Wheel 1: rich, slow, shallow, harmless, late, full, noisy, short, poor

Wheel 2: awake, hard, common, wet, weak, cheap, sad, ill

1. The _____**rich**_____ countries should help the _____**poor**_____ ones.

2. Don't stay up too _____ in the evening, if you have to get up _____ in the morning.

3. I told him I could only afford a _____ car, but he tried to sell me an _____ one.

4. I don't like _____ neighbours because I am a _____ person myself.

5. I got so _____ in the rain that it took an hour to get _____ again.

6. The water is quite _____ near the beach, but it gets _____ very quickly.

7. I said I wanted a _____–boiled egg, but they gave me one that was _____–boiled.

8. Basketball players are usually very _____ , you never see a _____ player.

9. Everybody had got up and was wide _____ , only Harold was still fast _____ .

10. I can't believe that Sue is _____ ; she was perfectly _____ when I last saw her.

11. A cobra can be _____ , but most snakes are quite _____ .

12. Eagles have become _____ in Europe, but blackbirds are quite _____ .

13. The train was rather _____ when we left, but after a couple of stops it got quite _____ .

14. I'm used to our old _____ car, John's Jaguar is much too _____ for me.

15. They say that a clown's _____ face quite often hides a _____ person.

16. Tom is used to _____ coffee, so Pam's espresso was much too _____ for him.

38

OPPOSITES

Pair up the words in the grey box with the words below to make antonym pairs.

| bottom | beginning | dwarf | entrance | friend | future | heaven | hope |
| love | morning | night | peace | problem | profit | question | victory |

answer _____   end _____   giant _____   past _____

day _____   enemy _____   hate _____   solution _____

defeat _____   evening _____   hell _____   top _____

despair _____   exit _____   loss _____   war _____

Fill in the blanks using the antonym pairs from above; you must use <u>both</u> words in each sentence.

1. The new boss took his company from a state of _____ into one of _____ .

2. With skilled leadership and clever tactics the general turned almost certain _____ into a great _____ .

3. We must forget about the _____ and look to the _____ .

4. Please drive in through the _____ to the car park and leave by the _____ .

5. James looked like a _____ standing beside Tom, a _____ of a man.

6. A treaty was signed at the end of the _____ in order to ensure _____ .

7. Just read this from the _____ and don't stop until you reach the _____ .

8. Their _____ of future happiness turned to _____ following the tragic accident.

9. Shopping, for some people, is their idea of _____ but for me it is _____ !

WHAT'S UP?

It is easy to understand 'up' when it means 'moving to a higher position: up the stairs, up the road' or 'being on or near the top of something: He lives up on that hill', but 'up' also turns up in many phrasal verbs (combinations of verb + adverb or preposition) which have an idiomatic meaning all of their own as in They broke up (separated) or He is washing up (cleaning the dishes).

All the verbs in the grey box can team up with 'up' to make up such phrasal verbs; use them to complete the sentences below, making sure you come up with the correct tense forms.

| catch | crack | fix | give | light | lock | look | make |
| mess | mix | pick | put | set | speak | warm | wind |

1. Di and Joan look so much alike that people always _____ them up.

2. Why don't you stay with us? We have a guest room and can easily _____ you up.

3. The inmates of this prison are all _____ up for the night.

4. Tom had started ten minutes earlier, but we soon _____ up with him.

5. You don't have to take a bus; I will _____ you up in my car.

6. Before a race an athlete needs to _____ up.

7. Sorry, this is a non-smoking area. You are not allowed to _____ up here.

8. I hate it when Tardy is so late. It always _____ up our plans.

9. I think Tim would have _____ up under the strain, if he hadn't left that job.

10. Please _____ up. I can't understand you.

11. Go and see the sports instructor. He will _____ you up with all the gear.

12. All those difficult words! I'll have to _____ them up in the dictionary.

13. Don't believe a word of what he says; I think he has just _____ up everything.

14. I have finally managed to _____ up smoking.

15. One good thing about digital watches is that you never have to _____ them up.

16. The government have _____ up a committee to look into the latest scandal.

IN A CLASS OF ITS OWN!

Example: Sparrow, owl, swan = Birds

Letters in the fat squares down = **The capital of a large country**

Rose, tulip, iris	=
Uncle, mother-in-law, cousin	=
Bee, ant, mosquito	=
Shirt, jeans, scarf	=
Europe, Asia, Australia	=
Chair, table, wardrobe	=
Carrot, cauliflower, celery	=
Oak, fir, chestnut	=
Great Britain, Italy, China	=
Earth, Neptune, Venus	=

Letters in the fat squares down = **What you can do when you want to improve your English**

Church, house, railway station	=
Lion, pig, elephant	=
Everest, Matterhorn, Etna	=
Suitcase, bag, trunk	=
Orange, pear, banana	=
Atlantic, Pacific	=
English, German, Chinese	=
Polo, chess, backgammon	=
London, Rome, Canterbury	=
Football, ice hockey, swimming	=
Red, mauve, green	=
Rhine, Thames, Danube	=
To call, to swim, to read	=
Theft, murder, fraud	=

  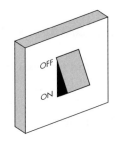

SHARED BEGINNINGS

Choose from the words in the grey box to complete the words in each group.

> book • bread • door • fire • hand • head • house
> land • life • **light** • milk • night • road • sun • water

light — bulb, house, switch

___ — place, man, arm

___ — boat, belt, style

___ — bag, shake, book

___ — bed, light, beam

___ — crumb, winner, bin

___ — mark, scape, slide

___ — club, dress, mare

___ — block, side, works

___ — bell, mat, step

___ — store, worm, mark

___ — man, shake, tooth

___ — colour, fall, front

___ — master, phones, line

___ — hold, maid, boat

EXERCISES

Fill in the blanks using words from the previous page.

A. 1. The new _____ makes an interesting _____ on the waterfront.

2. The newspaper _____ reported drugs found in a local _____ .

3. The _____ could not afford an extravagant _____ as he was the only _____ in his house.

4. The _____ left the milk on the _____ , out of the sun.

5. The bright _____ showed up the dust on the _____ beside the fireplace.

6. When the _____ rang she greeted her visitor with a _____ .

7. The Ritch family have a _____ to answer the _____ .

8. The _____ crew threw a _____ to the drowning man.

9. The roadworks to improve the motorway are proving to be a _____ for drivers.

B. A suntan is what you get <u>from the sun</u>, sunglasses protect your eyes <u>against the sun</u>, and sunrise is the <u>time</u> when the sun first appears in the sky. In each compound the 'shared beginning' contributes to the meaning in a different way. Choose five (or more) of the groups with a shared beginning and give a dictionary definition of each word.

_____
_____
_____
_____
_____
_____
_____
_____
_____

LANDMARKS

Reunite the famous international landmarks, countries and geographical features below by pairing up the missing words in the grey box with their first parts.

Africa	Delta	Highlands	Ness
Alps	Everest	Isles	Ocean
Canal	Falls	Liberty	Pole
Circle	Gibraltar	London	Rhine
Circus	Good Hope	Mountains	Wight

Loch _____

Mount _____

Niagara _____

Piccadilly _____

The River _____

The Tower of _____

The Swiss _____

The Atlantic _____

The British _____

The Cape of _____

The Isle of _____

The Mississippi _____

The North _____

The Panama _____

The Arctic _____

The Rocky _____

The Scottish _____

The Statue of _____

The Strait of _____

South _____

44

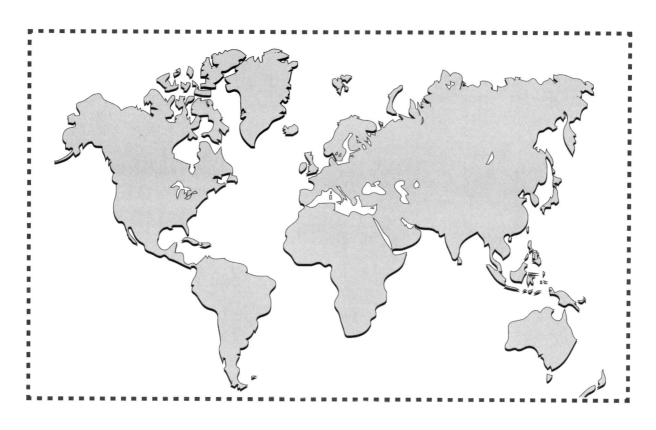

1. **Locate the landmarks – and others you may know – on the world map.**

2. **Now write one (or more) sentence(s) with each of the landmarks you have found.**

_____

_____

_____

_____

_____

_____

3. **Pool and compare your sentences in class and write a short description of the landmark together.**

_____

_____

_____

_____

_____

_____

_____

Animal Idioms

Straight from the Horse's Mouth

'Straight from the horse's mouth' is an **idiom** or **idiomatic expression:** an unusual combination of words, whose meaning you cannot understand from the individual words. English is very rich in such idiomatic expressions, many of them involve animals. Try to find out the meaning of the expressions below!

If you hear something *straight from the horse's mouth*,
- somebody talks to you in a very loud voice
- somebody has told you a lie
- you hear it from someone who is in a position to know it is true
- you read it in a magazine specialising in horse racing

Greg has *gone to the dogs*
- Greg has gone to the dog races
- Greg has let himself go morally or physically
- Greg has taken the dog for a walk to chat with other dog owners

DODO (extinct)

If something is *dead as a dodo*,
- it is no longer in fashion or no longer exists
- it is very boring
- it is very pale
- it is of very poor quality

If you've had *a whale of a time*
- you have enjoyed yourself very much
- you've been out to sea hunting whales
- you've had a busy day at the office
- you were drunk and now have a hangover

A *wolf in sheep's clothing* is
- a person who acts like a friend, but is hiding his unfriendly intentions
- somebody wearing the wrong sort of clothes
- a dangerous person dressed in woollen clothes
- a harmless person

When you *smell a rat*, you
- suspect something is wrong
- detect an unpleasant smell
- see an opportunity to make a lot of money

Sam had to do all the *donkey work* at his office
- Sam had to make the coffee for everybody at the office every day
- Sam had to do the least important and most unpleasant tasks at his office
- Sam tried to avoid all work

Renovating this house would be a *mammoth task*
- ❍ It is impossible
- ❍ It is a very large job needing a lot of effort
- ❍ It is not worth doing it
- ❍ It is too late, because mammoths are extinct

Sheila had *butterflies in her stomach*. She felt ...
- ❍ sick and tired of everything
- ❍ bored but content
- ❍ very happy
- ❍ nervous

Alf had other fish to fry
- ❍ Alf didn't like the fish and chips he was offered so he decided to fry his own
- ❍ Alf had other, more important things to do
- ❍ Alf had another helping of the fish and chips

If you *let the cat out of the bag*, you
- ❍ let the cat out of his sleeping bag to feed him
- ❍ give away a secret
- ❍ you have become a vegetarian and don't eat meat any more

Look what the cat's brought in!
- ❍ You are surprised and pleased to see someone!
- ❍ You are surprised at the number of mice your cat's brought in
- ❍ Your cat has been very naughty

If you *buy a pig in a poke*
- ❍ you buy a pig in an extra large box at the cattle market
- ❍ you have just landed a real bargain
- ❍ you buy something without seeing it or without knowing its value

Cheshire Cat

If you say that someone or something is *a sitting duck*, you mean that they
- ❍ are easy to attack or harm
- ❍ are difficult to move
- ❍ are lazy and phlegmatic

Grandfather grinned like a Cheshire cat
- ❍ He smiled nervously
- ❍ He had a wide smile all over his face
- ❍ He smiled at his new cat from Cheshire

If somebody *makes a pig of himself*, he
- ❍ only thinks of eating ham
- ❍ is stubborn and unreasonable
- ❍ is clever and knows how to protect his interests
- ❍ eats far too much and greedily

Making a beeline for something means
- ❍ to go quickly or by the shortest way towards something
- ❍ taking your time to go somewhere, but getting there in the end
- ❍ having to stand in a queue to be served in the restaurant

Look in the Right Place

You'll find a doctor in a hospital, and a teacher in a . . .

Divide into two teams. Pair up the words that belong together in each column.

1	article	_____	aeroplane
2	teacher	_____	bathroom
3	waiter	_____	car
4	seat belt	_____	kitchen
5	violinist	_____	office
6	shower	_____	circus
7	clown	_____	prison
8	page	_____	airport
9	altar	_____	palace
10	cook	_____	orchestra
11	transit lounge	_____	book
12	secretary	_____	restaurant
13	cell	_____	church
14	actor	_____	newspaper
15	king	_____	school
16	pilot	_____	theatre

48

FALLING INTO PLACE

Look in the grey box and see who or what else you could find in the 'right places'.

acrobat	cooker	headline	musician	speedometer
blackboard	dashboard	headmaster	photocopier	stage
box office	departure gate	illustration	vicar	steering wheel
check-in counter	dessert trolley	index	pulpit	throne
cockpit	editorial	inmate	ringmaster	towel rail
congregation	filing cabinet	lion-tamer	saucepan	warden
conductor	flight attendant	menu	servants	washbasin

AEROPLANE _____

PRISON _____

AIRPORT _____

NEWSPAPER _____

BATHROOM _____

OFFICE _____

BOOK _____

ORCHESTRA _____

CAR _____

PALACE _____

CHURCH _____

RESTAURANT _____

CIRCUS _____

SCHOOL _____

KITCHEN _____

THEATRE _____

49

Don't count your chickens...

'*Don't count your chickens before they're hatched*' is a **proverb**. The English often use proverbs and pro-verbial expressions in their daily lives. Proverbs are used to give a word of warning or advice or as a comment on a situation. Some can be simple folk sayings, others more philosophical or metaphorical. Try to find out the meaning of the proverbs below!

If you put the cart before the horse, you
- use the wrong kind of vehicle to get somewhere
- deal with things in the wrong order
- like the cart much better than the horse
- have done something wrong and regret it

Don't count your chickens before they're hatched!
- Don't provoke people!
- Don't be over-optimistic or over-confident of success!
- Don't expect too many chicken before they're hatched!
- Don't be too optimistic about getting a chance to dance with young girls at the party

If you have too many irons in the fire, you
- try to iron too many clothes at the same time
- are involved in too many different activities at the same time
- have too many household gadgets
- have put too many irons in the fireplace

You can't teach an old dog new tricks!
- Your dog is too old to learn new tricks
- Some people, especially old people, don't like to try new ways of doing things
- Your husband is more fond of the family dog than his family and nothing will make him change his feelings

A leopard never changes its spots, means
- that somebody's basic nature never changes
- a person who never changes his or her clothes
- a person who always wears spotty clothes

You can take a horse to water, but you cannot make him drink
- Horses are stubborn animals with a will of their own
- Don't rely on other people, but do things yourself
- You can try to convince or persuade people, but you cannot force them to do something they don't want to do

MAKE YOUR OWN DEFINITIONS!

Look at the proverbs below. Now get into two groups – A and B. Take the proverbs for your group and write 3 definitions – two false, one true – for each proverb to test the skills of your fellow pupils. Score 10 points for each proverb they don't decipher. If you are unsure ask your teacher for the correct definition.

GROUP A

1. Learn to walk before you run.

2. It never rains but it pours.

3. You can't have your cake and eat it.

4. Many hands make light work.

GROUP B

1. Look before you leap.

2. All that glitters is not gold.

3. A burnt child dreads the fire.

4. Better be safe than sorry.

Look for Links

| Day is to sun as night is to | ○ dawn | ✖ moon | ○ sleep | ○ dusk |

Choose the correct word to complete the sentences as in the example above.

1. Hunger is to eat as thirst is to ○ water ○ drink ○ tea ○ dry
2. Leather is to shoe as wool is to ○ sheep ○ needles ○ jumper ○ shirt
3. Sight is to eyes as smell is to ○ mouth ○ feet ○ glasses ○ nose
4. Leg is to knee as arm is to ○ wrist ○ elbow ○ fingers ○ shoulders
5. Aunt is to niece as uncle is to ○ girl ○ sister ○ nephew ○ boy
6. Roof is to house as ceiling is to ○ wall ○ floor ○ building ○ room
7. Cat is to animal as fly is to ○ fish ○ insect ○ human ○ bird
8. Ear is to hear as eye is to ○ nose ○ face ○ hand ○ see
9. Man is to foot as cat is to ○ paw ○ collar ○ whiskers ○ tail
10. Opera is to sing as theatre is to ○ dance ○ comedy ○ act ○ play
11. Woman is to wife as man is to ○ father ○ husband ○ boy ○ gentleman
12. Light is to dark as happy is to ○ ill ○ content ○ friendly ○ sad
13. Cat is to kitten as horse is to ○ puppy ○ foal ○ kid ○ lamb
14. Wood is to tree as wool is to ○ sheep ○ sweater ○ shirt ○ cow
15. Bread is to baker as clothes are to ○ wardrobe ○ shirts ○ model ○ tailor
16. Pig is to grunt as cow is to ○ bark ○ moo ○ bleat ○ neigh

FILL THAT GAP

Form words by supplying as many letters as you wish.
Words with 3 Letters = 3 Points; 4 Letters = 4 Points; 5 Letters = 5 Points; 6 Letters = 6 Points; 7 and more Letters: 10 Points

_____ et	_____ at	_____ ill
_____ et	_____ at	_____ ill
_____ et	_____ at	_____ ill
_____ et	_____ at	_____ ill
_____ et	_____ at	_____ ill
_____ et	_____ at	_____ ill
_____ et	_____ at	_____ ill
_____ et	_____ at	_____ ill
_____ et	_____ at	_____ ill
_____ et	_____ at	_____ ill
_____ et	_____ at	_____ ill

Score: _____   **Score:** _____   **Score:** _____

Keep going!

Better!

Very good!

Brilliant!

★ **Write sentences of your own involving at least ten of the words above.**

53

Sounds Interesting!

We English are a funny lot
500 000 words we've got
and spell the ones that sound the same
in different ways – eternal shame!
And words with selfsame spelling hold
pronunciations dozenfold.

It's through and brew, but hard and ward
It's bird and heard, but word and sword.
Read rhymes with lead and lead with red
and read with bed and so does said.

And the maker of a verse
Cannot rhyme his horse with worse.
Beard sounds not the same as heard,
Cord is different from word,
Cow is cow, but low is low,
Shoe is never rhymed with toe.
And since pay is rhymed with say,
Why not paid with said, I pray?
Wherefore done, but gone and lone?
Is there any reason known?

Why deer and dear, but beer and bear
and meet and meat, and fare and fair?
Peers and pears and stares and stairs
and here and there make funny pairs!

A show is not a show in shower
nor fat in father, flow in flower.
Consider dearth and great and threat
they rhyme with worth and eight and debt.
Foul is to soul like howl to hole
and sour to shower like role to bowl.

And, in short, it seems to me –
Sounds and letters disagree.

VEXING VOWELS

The vowel combination 'ea' is pronounced in many different ways in English. Take the words in the grey box and put them into the correct category.

| appeal | beard | bread | breakfast | breath | cheat | clear | ear | early | earn |
| earth | east | fear | feather | health | heard | peace | pearl | real | sea |

ea

beat / iː /	hear / ɪə /	head / ɛ /	learn / ɜː /

Many words which contain the same sounds are often spelled quite differently. Find the words with the same vowel sounds and write them into the correct category and add any others you can think of.

| beer | bell | bird | burn | dead | dear | deer | feet | flea | heap |
| herd | here | hurt | niece | piece | pier | red | said | tread | word |

beat / iː /	hear / ɪə /	head / ɛ /	learn / ɜː /

It's not what you say...
IT'S How YOU SAY IT!

English is very rich in verbal substitutes that can be used as an alternative to *'said'* after direct speech; they make the report on what was said more lively, colourful and interesting and are therefore valuable tools for novelists, journalists and everybody who wants to write good English.

Pair up the verbs in the grey box with the sentences on the left; use a dictionary for words you don't know.

admitted	announced	apologised	asked	boasted
commanded	complained	concluded	decided	exclaimed
shouted	volunteered	vowed	warned	whispered

1. 'Oh, I'm very sorry,' Tom _____.

2. 'Where did you buy that nice car?' my friend _____.

3. 'I can dance better than Michael Jackson,' Clum C. _____.

4. 'Hey, you! Get out of my garden,' the man _____.

5. 'I will always love you,' the husband _____.

6. 'This music is much too loud,' the neighbours _____.

7. 'This man was poisoned,' Sherlock Holmes _____.

8. 'It was me who broke that cup,' Sabrina _____.

9. 'Pssst! Don't wake up the baby,' she _____.

10. 'Don't touch that cat. It will scratch you,' Melissa _____.

11. 'Right then, I will take the green sofa,' Mr. Smith _____.

12. 'Good Heavens, a genuine Rubens painting,' the art collector _____.

13. 'You will stay here till six o'clock,' the officer _____.

14. 'We will write the test on Tuesday,' the teacher _____.

15. 'I will wash the car for you,' Anthony _____.

Put words into the mouths of these persons – look at their faces and think of what they might be saying.

Supply sentences that go with the reporting verbs. Their number, of course, is only limited by your imagination.

1. '_____,' the child begged.

2. '_____,' Dad promised.

3. '_____?' the reporter wanted to know.

4. '_____,' he accepted.

5. '_____,' the expert predicted.

6. '_____,' Ryan suggested.

7. '_____,' the teacher warned Keith.

8. '_____,' my father groaned.

9. '_____,' the doctor explained.

10. '_____,' Tony offered.

11. '_____,' he gulped.

12. '_____,' mother reminded us.

13. '_____,' the policeman reported.

14. '_____,' the detective assured the old lady.

15. '_____,' the pilot informed the passengers.

SCRABBLE

Form as many words as possible with the letters below. Write down the sum of the value points of the letters you used. You can use each letter only once with each word. If you can use all the letters to form a word you get an extra bonus of 20 points.

A₁ C₃ R₂ E₁ H₂ E₁ T₁

Words	Points	Words	Points	Words	Points	Words	Points
						TOTAL Points:	

C₃ I₁ R₂ N₁ E₁ T₁ A₁

Words	Points	Words	Points	Words	Points	Words	Points
						TOTAL Points:	

I₁ A₁ X₅ N₁ E₂ M₂ E₁

Words	Points	Words	Points	Words	Points	Words	Points
						TOTAL Points:	

Eight Letter Scrabble

Form as many words as possible with the letters below. Write down the sum of the value points of the letters you used. You can use each letter only once with each word. If you can use all the letters to form a word you get a bonus of 20 points. Here is a tip: the first all-letter-word is something one likes to go to, the second someone you wouldn't like to meet, the third is something you can eat.

A₁ T₁ S₁ F₂ I₁ L₂ E₁ V₃

Words	Points	Words	Points	Words	Points	Words	Points
							TOTAL Points:

A₁ R₂ C₂ M₂ I₁ L₂ I₁ N₁

Words	Points	Words	Points	Words	Points	Words	Points
							TOTAL Points:

B₂ G₂ E₁ T₁ A₁ E₁ L₂ V₃

Words	Points	Words	Points	Words	Points	Words	Points
							TOTAL Points:

Be as good as your word

Choose the correct word to complete these sentences.

1. Ray has no money. He is _____ . ○ blank   ○ broke   ○ mean
2. Let me _____ your bag for you. ○ carry   ○ wear   ○ bear
3. London has about 7 million _____ . ○ burghers   ○ inhabitants   ○ folk
4. She is going to _____ coffee for all of us. ○ cook   ○ boil   ○ make
5. When you buy something you often get a _____ . ○ deposit   ○ receipt   ○ bill
6. Vegetarians don't eat _____ . ○ flesh   ○ meat   ○ beef
7. Nobody is perfect. We all make _____ . ○ mistakes   ○ failures   ○ faults
8. Dad is always on time. He's so _____ . ○ punctilious   ○ punctual   ○ timely
9. We went to see a football _____ yesterday. ○ match   ○ game   ○ play
10. Dad has no hair on his head. He is _____ . ○ bold   ○ hairless   ○ bald
11. The Rhine is Germany's longest _____ . ○ river   ○ flood   ○ stream
12. Anne can't hear. She is _____ . ○ dumb   ○ blind   ○ deaf
13. She wears a gold _____ on her wrist. ○ clock   ○ alarm clock   ○ watch
14. Can you _____ me to play the piano? ○ learn   ○ teach   ○ assist
15. Could you _____ me a pound, please? ○ borrow   ○ lend   ○ loan
16. Let's have a _____ for lunch! ○ pause   ○ interval   ○ break

BE EVEN BETTER THAN YOUR WORD!

Fill in the blanks to show that you have also understood the meaning of some of the alternative words. Use your dictionary for help if necessary.

1. Her face went _____**blank**_____ (= showing no expression or feeling).

2. I really love to _____ pure woollen jumpers.

3. The pillar has to be strong enough to _____ the weight of the roof.

4. When the water starts to _____ you can add the pasta.

5. She paid a _____ towards the cost of her new car.

6. Although there was lots of blood it was only a _____ wound and James suffered no serious injury.

7. A power _____ caused the town to be plunged into darkness.

8. When her father saw the costly phone bill, Jane decided to make a _____ exit.

9. As it was raining we stayed indoors and played a _____ of cards.

10. The _____ soldier went into battle showing no signs of fear.

11. When the river began to _____ some people had to leave their homes.

12. She was struck _____ with fright and couldn't utter a word.

13. In our lounge we have a large gold _____ on the mantelpiece.

14. It's not easy to _____ a new language.

15. May I _____ £5 if I promise to repay it tomorrow?

16. She seems to talk and talk without taking a _____ for breath.

17. During the _____ we went for a drink in the theatre bar.

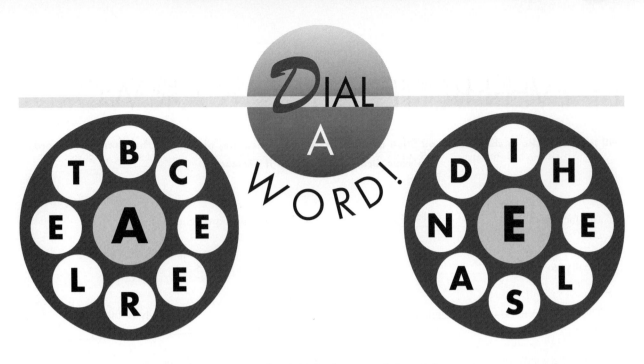

Dial A Word!

Form words with the letters of the dial.
The words must contain the letter shown in the middle of the dial. You get more points for longer words.

3 Letters = 1 Point; 4 Letters = 2 Points; 5 Letters = 3 Points; 6 Letters = 4 Points; More = 5 Points; All: 12 Points

3 Letters _____

4 Letters _____

5 Letters _____

6 Letters _____

More _____

All Letters _____

SCORE _____

3 Letters _____

4 Letters _____

5 Letters _____

6 Letters _____

More _____

All Letters _____

SCORE _____

FAMOUS *L*AST WORDS

Divide into two teams. Group letters around the vowels to form words.
4 Letters = 2 Points; 5 = 3 Points; 6 = 4 Points; 7 = 5 Points; 8 = 6 Points; More = 10 Points

_____ oo _____	_____ ee _____	_____ ie _____
_____ oo _____	_____ ee _____	_____ ie _____
_____ oo _____	_____ ee _____	_____ ie _____
_____ oo _____	_____ ee _____	_____ ie _____
_____ oo _____	_____ ee _____	_____ ie _____
_____ oo _____	_____ ee _____	_____ ie _____
_____ oo _____	_____ ee _____	_____ ie _____
_____ oo _____	_____ ee _____	_____ ie _____
_____ oo _____	_____ ee _____	_____ ie _____
_____ oo _____	_____ ee _____	_____ ie _____

Score: _____ **Score:** _____ **Score:** _____

Form words by supplying as many letters as you wish.
Words with 4 Letters = 3 Points; 5 Letters = 4 Points; 6 Letters = 6 Points; 7 and more Letters: 10 Points

Keep going!

Better!

Very good!

Brilliant!

_____ ay	_____ ate	_____ eat
_____ ay	_____ ate	_____ eat
_____ ay	_____ ate	_____ eat
_____ ay	_____ ate	_____ eat
_____ ay	_____ ate	_____ eat
_____ ay	_____ ate	_____ eat
_____ ay	_____ ate	_____ eat
_____ ay	_____ ate	_____ eat
_____ ay	_____ ate	_____ eat
_____ ay	_____ ate	_____ eat
_____ ay	_____ ate	_____ eat

Score: _____ **Score:** _____ **Score:** _____